"Vulnerable, visceral, meditative"
~Maggie Smith, Good Bones

GIVE A GIRL CHAOS

{see what she can do}

Heidi Seaborn

Mastodon Publishing
Thoughts Made Real

First Edition
1 2 3 4 5 6 7 8 9

Cover art by Rachel Kelli
Interior design by Rachel Kelli and Mandi Manns

Copyright ©2019 Heidi Seaborn
Library of Congress Cataloging-in-Publication Data

ISBN: 978-1-7320091-4-1
Library of Congress Control Number: 2018956227

Mastodon Publishing
Thoughts Made Real
mastodonpublishing.com

For special discounted bulk purchases, please contact:
Mastodon Publishing sales@mastodonpublishing.com

To book events, readings, and author signings, please contact:
info@mastodonpublishing.com

For my parents who raised me in a loving and glorious way and gave me the power to harness chaos, and for Jack, Hallie, Nicky and Scott for becoming my universe.

TABLE OF CONTENTS

GIVE A GIRL CHAOS

Chaos arrives screaming—born
                              under a certain star   shifting
                                      every day that follows
Chaos
              is an unplanned dinner party
              the neighbors stop by for a drink   and never leave

Chaos   lives in homes
                      in bottles   stashed   in the linen closet

                      in dreams
                              when the lights go out
                                      and families turn upon themselves
Chaos is cancer
              rooting our bodies' richest soil

Chaos   never
                      travels light   overpacks   overstays
                                              delays departures
Chaos—
              another name for a dark heart
                              roaming
                                      back alleys of our world

seas rise   maelstroms slash
                      skies seethe
                              fires spark   spread

O she is hungry these days
                              this goddess of Chaos   this mother

once a girl who dreamed big
a girl who birthed a universe

                      imagine what she could do now

1

a girl who harnesses Chaos
      can whip   winds into a horde
                                 of butterflies
      hush hurricanes   settle
      storms   salve spirits

O give a girl a little Chaos
        see what she can do

Don't bother to knock come on in
    you are meant to be here

             sometimes
               Chaos is the way in.

WEATHER

Suppose you wake up to his weather
and find yourself bruised by his weather.

Under 600 thread-count sheets,
another morning pursued by his weather.

Silence eludes the hunter. You play opossum.
He slips on a charcoal gray suit—his weather.

Your body knifes into the mattress,
eyes shut & nerves cued to his weather.

Even in the kitchen, slicing a peach,
weighted air exudes his weather,

burns the morning's coffee, scalding
your tongue—now muted by his weather.

Out the window, the sky loses all color
to black, smeared tar of his weather.

Rain dints the house roof percussive
& thunder clears its throat like his weather.

As another storm gathers, day
& night fuse at the horizon—his weather

into a fist, borne by the sea, blowing
your way. You steady for his weather.

AFTER THE BATTLES

~Húmera, Pozuela de Alarcón, near Madrid, Spain, 2007. The setting for two battles during the Spanish Civil War in 1936-1937, shortly after Federico García Lorca was assassinated.

Querido Federico,

My camellias blossom in winter,
blood red petals
I cup in my palm, bruising
the blossoms brown.
Earth vein of violence seething
from Las Batallas de la Carretera de la Coruña,
when Franco's mercenary soldiers, seeing
no sun in late November, dug into this hill
that now holds our home—*scarred-over wounds.*
We too sharpen our bayonets against stone.

~

Poets marched to Húmera—
José, León, Rafael, Miguel—your comrades.
Rafael Alberti walked out from Madrid,
across the Rio Manzanares, into Casa de Campo
in the Republicans' boot steps.
They lifted his lyrics to the fire that night.

~

We shiver at sunrise, ready for Christmas.
My husband's words scud near my ear.
I finger the table linen's holly berry embroidery.
He drags his tongue in brandy,
carves my flesh from bone.
   We lived a hundred years inside a knife.

~

6

Fog settled here on the second battle.
December's like that. Ghosts dropping
their winter cloaks across the land—

~

I sleep the sleep of heavy weather,
wrapped in fog's cashmere.
My battles—my husband's knife
jabs the space between us—

~

Federico,
when Spain splintered,
you splintered. Broken

raw earth beneath olive trees
      burdened with green fruit,
      refusing to fall.
Against a red earth cemetery wall,
red souls shot, red blood
      blackening red soil.

Your verses buried with the second shot
to your head, sonnet on your lips.

~

The dead wear wings of moss.
Living, I search for feathers, gossamer,
silk, sailcloth to stitch a flight.
To soar beyond these *fields of ancient blood,*
away from threats of death breathing
in the bed beside me.

~

My days. Your dark sonnets.
I weigh stones, oranges against heart, hands,
deadbolt the door to my husband,
to what comes next.

The blown sky, moon and I
stay up all night, counting scars.
Your meteor flashes.
The burning tail of ghazals remains.

STUNG

I stirred the hornet's nest,
shears cutting into the brush.

Disturbing the murmur of day,
I stand still, wait out their frantic flight.

Like when I told my then-husband
"I don't love you," maybe never had,

over a birthday dinner. Sunset's glaze
reflected off the gold earrings

he'd bought me in Cairo.
He too must have glowed,

until I spoke the words that buzzed
around his head, pulled at the fragile

papery nest of our marriage. Now
prune the underbrush to plant anew.

AT THE END OF OUR MARRIAGE,
YOU CONTRACT CONGESTIVE HEART FAILURE

Your heart wants to die—
muscles stiffen for the final blows.
Each thick chamber pushing blood like a broom
slowly, while I move from room to room ghosting
what remains.
Then your walls weaken.
Paint peels off rotted plaster.

Your kidneys kick in to hold water
    Remember hiking the Hollywood Reservoir
      with the kids, sun setting, coyotes calling, gates locked?
and salt. I floated the Dead Sea,
the Great Salt Lake of your body—

now swamped. I row away,
stop, throw a short line *catch it* I shout.
Your busted heart the last hold on my own.

HOW TO HOLD A HEART

~Instructions to a cardiac surgeon.

Weighing ten ounces, the heart feels unexpectedly heavy.
An organ you could palm, but don't, as it is slippery
with blood and the surprise of pulsing. Pulsing
even later, as you lay it in a stainless-steel basin.

So best to use two hands.
Hook your cupped palms together,
linking the pinkies, to create a basket
cradling the dislodged and beating heart.

What will you do as it bleeds out?
Turn your back, ready the not-so-new new heart
as the nurse whisks away the old to the fire.
Or do you blink your eyes closed
long enough for inhale, exhale.

Long enough to consider him as your hand unfurls,
fingers graze his shoulder, assess his condition:
neither dead nor alive, heartless,
free from the expectation to love,
to be that perfect someone, that one and only.

SE/PARA/TION

Weekends he walks
      past the house   into the barn drags
          a rototiller out   tugs on work gloves
      turns the soil black as the coffee
      she cradles over the sink   watching.

IMMOLATION

In the middle of our divorce
you fled
              to Tunisia.

Not next door   not
              the town over
Tunisia

        as Arab Spring smoldered—
loosely packed pine needles sparked
by North African sun.

Could you feel it
              walking
through November 7 Square

scattering young men   like startled doves

to cluster in cafés   untouched espresso
                 and cigarette smoke?

You wanted that too—

        let the match
        burn down
        singe your fingertips white
                follow its flame to my ash.

STOP MOTION

~After a photo of frozen monarch butterflies taken in Michoacán, Mexico

Once in Santa Cruz
      hundreds of monarchs swirled
            around me
                  flirted
                with eyelashes   fingers
then flew to Mexico.

Clutter of paper tigers

                      spread across a canvas of snow.

Wings fanned in all directions   frozen
                        in flight.

Sometimes we fail to see the signs—
don't   not now   maybe never
     drive when you're tired
     walk alone at night
     marry that man.

We fly into cold weather
                wings of persimmon

                      gold   flash.

HOW TO RUN AWAY

Pack light. One change of clothes,
toothbrush, comb, headlamp, a book
shoved into your day bag.

Lift the worn duvet, slip from the bed.
The floor's cold sets you in motion.
Pull on your stashed clothes, coat, boots,
shrug the pack over your shoulder.

Leave the room
of the man sleeping roughly next to you,
the crackle and hint of lingering smoke,
from a winter fire smoldering the hearth,
the whispered story.

Don't look back. Don't hesitate hand on door.
Once outside, walk with the certainty
of a postman on his route.

Take only
that evening and not what followed,
not the days and nights stretched
and burdened by grief's tonnage.

Disappear into the land,
the crowd you shun. Assimilate,
change color, shed skins, wear hats.
Cross borders, city, county, country. Cross
into a place, a space foreign. Forgotten.

CROSSING THE DEAD SEA

I'm bleeding, hunched roadside.
I thought I could walk
from Jerusalem to Eilat.
A Bedouin offers tea.
His palms the color of sand
cup warm clay bowls of steeped
habuck marmaraya cardamom.

I'd left Jerusalem on Easter
Sunday—third night of Pesach.
Robed sandal-footed clergy parading Jesus,
shtreimel-hatted *Haredi* Jews ducking in
and out of shops, wives herding children.

Beyond the Bedouin's tent flap,
Jordanian border patrols stand
in relief against an ochre sky, the Dead Sea.

Warm water stings like nettles.
I float like the dead,
lick salt crust off my arms

My body is charcoal with mud.
As it dries, I scan the horizon
for Israeli soldiers patrolling,
but the sun blots distance.
The Dead Sea washes
mud away, decades of mud,
leaving camps hemmed
with barbed wire
pinning the Iraqi border.
I crossed a border coming here.

WITH THE MAASAI

When the rains fail,
they fail again. Tanzania burns
dry. Ntimama curses the empty
sky. His beasts, bones.
Tanzania burns dry. Parched
plains diminish
beasts, just bones. The empty
sky steals grain, milk, meat,

flesh to bone. Cattle
wander with wildebeest
as Tanzania burns dry as stone.
Ntimama curses this land:

water dried to mud, mud
dried to blood red. Rift
Valley, earth and gash.
Cattle, then children.

Small bones burned, dry.
Cursed by this empty
sky, the gash of withered
earth, when the rains fail and fail.

EARTHQUAKE

I have a room   follow me

the room has blue curtains
outhouse across the garden

the earthquake   heaves   me out of bed
rolls   my body   into the rubble   of morning broken

within the   crumbled   walls   wine from a shop runs
                down a sloping street
                                to the Adriatic Sea
splintered glass
            a boy   crying
                        his body quiets with my hold

aftershocks rumble for half a century

POSTCARD/Dubrovnik, Yugoslavia 25.04.79

TRAVEL ADVISORY FOR TURKEY

I will not snake the Spice Bazaar maze in Istanbul,
past the sacks of psychedelic colored *baharat* and herbs.
I won't inhale cumin, sumac, saffron and mint.
I will not bring home *tuzlu* nuts and Turkish Delight
or know the bolt of *Arabica* coffee sipped from a demitasse
with a bite of *beyaz peynir* cheese.

I will not heed the imam call to prayers,
look to the minarets to guide me to the Sultanahmet mosque,
wrap my pashmina over my head, shoulders, slip off my shoes,
find my place among the women,
stand, kneel, touch my head to carpet, stand.
The prayers a requiem for the dead, the dying.

I will not haggle with the rug dealer as he and his cousins
roll open another hand-knotted Anatolian carpet, blood
red, starred with indigo and gold blossoms.
"This one. Ma'am, this one best for you."
It will not arrive on my doorstep months later
wrapped in burlap, unfurling a scent of *shisha* smoke.

I will not see girls, braids bouncing as they skip
to the jump rope's beat, the sing-song song.
Boys dribbling, rising to layup, block an imaginary basket.
The ball tapping from outstretched hand to hand,
skittering off down the dirt alley, mothers pulling
aside curtain doorways to scold.

I will not eat charred sheep *kebaps*
or drink *rati* and pick *lüfer* off the bone by the Bosphorus
imagining Ottoman trading ships navigating its length.
I will not journey to the Hattusas
as the sun illuminates history, stories, what remains
from thieves, Pergamon's curators, ancient battles

like this war: the remnant of an Imperial tapestry,
a lost province, gaming foreign powers, the Euphrates
knotted near the border, its mouth burned dry.

EGYPTIAN ERASURE

~From Ahmed M. Abul Ella Ali's blog

January 28, 2011

one million   march

Tahrir Square

son Basil me

cross   the Nile

tear gas   rubber

police   ambush

don't   die Daddy

blinded   shot

run

crowds surge

strange night,   prison   opened

terror

February 2, 2011

people   on horseback   camels

swords   guns

300 people die

—martyrs

24

February 8, 2011

              my mother   cried
millions   army   down

February 11, 2011

    crowds
                siege.
                       Mubarak   gone.

DISSIDENT

It took 30 seconds. The driver's head cranked to reverse the bus, I leaned forward as if in prayer, then slipped my cool arm over the seat in front of mine, slid the thick worn paperback book down, my fingers brushing ever so briefly against the teacher's thin blue cotton shirt. Sensing it, he settled back, his balding head crowning the seat. At the museum, Mr. Horváth wore a brown corduroy jacket as he guided us, sweat gathering like dew along his hairline. He took off his glasses, rubbed them with a handkerchief, looked at me, gave a half-smile, then turned.

BEHIND THE WALL

We walk eyes steady
between walls of soldiers
and into winter.

Ashen-clouded skies
darken stone monuments
crowned with barbed wire.

Silent line waiting
for potato soup, dry bread.
We eat with mittens on.

ÂME EN PEINE À PARIS

Paris written down my naked arms,
shimmering seam of truth and lies,
ghosts sip espresso in café bars.

Along the Seine, peonies float, stars
of pink petals reflect the clotted sky,
shadows written down my naked arms.

Wooden boats, a sepia pond far
from the boy with lashed, dusk eyes.
Ghosts sip espresso in café bars,

suck *les huîtres* off the shell, carve
steak from bone with silver knives,
Paris is written down my naked arms.

In caverns beneath speeding cars,
red dress swirls away Paris's demise,
ghosts sipping espresso in café bars.

Paris's shimmering seam: river of stars,
succor, *sucre* for *Ars*
Poetica written down my naked arms,
I sip espresso with ghosts in café bars.

BEFORE AND AFTER

~For Jyamjung Bhote Sherpa Salaka after the Ghorka earthquake.

Sunrise slivers through ice. Trail carved from snow and rock. Cold thin breaths swallowed like yak dung smoke, sweat of men sleeping head-to-toe in the kitchen. As we left Leboche, we knew to follow you. Footmarks in dust, mud, snow. We climbed Everest's high valleys. Now you guide us by motorbike past hand-tilled Newari farms into Kathmandu's dusty hive, beneath stone temples breathing pigeons, filmy young men gathered on steps, down an earthen alley, through metal gates, upstairs to your home. Chere steams *momos,* stirs *dal baht,* your children carve fragile smiles.

Beneath Himalayas
plum-robed monks
bury prayer bird-less skies

BEYOND

Our bed smells of coconut milk. Outside
    the tide washes through splay-fingered
        mangrove roots, leaving a lacy stitch

with each wave
    as a fisherman heaves
        his longboat onto the beach.

An acacia tree shades
    the gardenia bush beside
        this pink house on stilts,
           salt air.

A boy riding a lemon-colored motorbike
    drops boxes of peppers
        at the kitchen door.
           Across the road,
the sign stabbed
    into the grass warns
        Entering Tsunami
        Hazard Zone

Edging the jungle,
    a golden girl
        nests in the pungent
           branches of a mango tree.
She sees beyond
    the ocean's edge,
        the earth curving away,
           pulling the tide like a blanket.

IN MEMORIAM

Swallowed by a fire
that skipped borders,
shouldered roads, bridged
rivers, flicked, flamed, licked its way across
ranches, farms and fishing cabins,
leaving a black streak like tar
smeared by the hand of God.

Scorched ponderosa trees remain
blackened fingers in the cloudless sky.
Fields of flamboyant pink fireweed bloom
from gnarled, charred hunks and seared earth.
Wild roses, chaparral
grow beneath clutches of aspens.
Light sifts through ripe green leaves.

POSTCARD/*Chewach River Valley, Okanaogan Co., WA 25.08.16*

GET OUT

Spotted owls are the first to go, heeding heat's blush,

warning goldfinch, warblers, woodpeckers,

chickadees, wrens, sparrows. Even ash-throated thrush

disappear before ash falls, leaving only predators—eagles,

hawks—who dive through smoke to hover

above scampering

rabbits and mice.

White-throated sparrow, migration hardwired to time and place,
know to fly ahead of hurricane's landfall.

While whimbrels fly through, threading the hurricane's vacant eye—
a winged tight wire—
and chimney swifts shift off to France.

Canopy stripped, Puerto Rican parrots disappear
along with Cozumel thrashers and terns
into ether.

Fifteen minutes before an earthquake, ravens

blacken the sky as if a silent gun's been fired.

When the moon eclipses the sun, whippoorwills flash awake,
meadowlarks, finches and dark-eyed juncos hush their song.

Leave the perfect sycamore tree, honeyed nectar bush,

beetle bountiful woods, wheat brushed hills—

danger

fly away fly away fly away fly   fly   fly   fly
                                              away.

WANDERING SEEDS

On knees rooting morning glory
        tangled beneath hydrangeas
                I'm at my garden wall, cursing

the Edo Japanese for cultivating morning glory. Rainbows of tissue
blossoms bloomed open, umbrellas under a shogun sun, their vines
anchoring an island of people in walled gardens.

The Ottomans edged
north along the Red Sea
cupping the green Mediterranean
to a thirsty mouth
then flowed into Danube's blue vein—

Europeans stamped *New* onto each settlement and Galileo cast his
sights further yet, tethering the stars that lit up seas like garden lights

to guide ships
        carrying morning glory seeds
                to my soil
                        to strangle my dahlias
                                choke my pear espalier
                                        my wall.

I HAD TRAVELLED FAR ENOUGH
~An ekphrastic of "Nothing Lasts Forever" by the artist Kelly O'Dell

I had travelled far enough.
    Knew to dig my fingernail through skin,

winnow a slight tag

to tug, deftly rend

rind from fruit, slowly,

a ribbon. Even so, the white
    membrane caught, tore

the fruit, bleeding
        juice my fingers
luring bees to leave the sweet
    gardenia alone.

Hum a house by the sea.

Finches nest
    in an orange tree.
Inside, a woman nurses a baby.

The lighthouse flares orange,
        guiding
the image
    burned onto my body

as I peel skin
    from membrane
        from heart.

CRASH

~My mother, sisters, brother, me and the man that hit us, August 1967

My hand slipping wheel
lost in thought
Marilyn telling me she's pregnant
this baby as I climb in my truck
pull out our driveway
head to work this baby
as I run the stop sign
by the Congregational church
this baby
I slam into a station wagon
this baby
jump out run
children mother
daughter—I reach for her

My hand slipping wheel arm thrusting
over back to hold Heidi
I see her body fold
door curving around her like a baseball glove
an explosion of glass
slowed to one strobe flash staccato
Even now decades later
I don't see the truck that hit us
I see Heidi I don't hear her or Page
Muffie Stevie in the back
I hear the crash then glass—
glinty as wind.

Hurt
don't know why
hurt
in Mom's eyes,
look away glass

splinters cover me
like field burrs
door shoved hard
my hip   man
reaching
broken window
he has glasses
he yells *alright, you?*
nothing
but *owowowowowow*
tomorrow—
tweeze glass
from body leaving
fields of bloody stars

Muffie slammed into me
screaming   my legs Page legs
something bad   a jumble Mom says
I fell off the back seat Muffie   when we sleep in the same bed
on top of me   Mom says *are you*
playing horse   *all right*
a sticky lemon drop   *are you all right*
I can't reach   we are hiding
my hands are somewhere   I've lost my glasses
Heidi's hurt   Stevie's
                                                            flying

I'm flying!   flying
                       from the way way back

        I'm an astronaut
                              my orange life vest
                       flying over seats

        my sisters

My super-hero life vest

when my sisters chased me off the dock
I floated

now I fly

How much I loved that station wagon, blueberry blue, Coppertone and popsicle. I had painted a red stripe along each side. Jaunty I thought. Maybe the red stripe invited the truck: slip the stop; follow this line like a vein into the car, my children. I don't remember where we were going— I remember Heidi, her blue eyes opened into the sky.

WHAT I KNEW

about the war I knew
from the tv black & white & gray.
Knew nothing about green
blotting the sun jungle green
slick as seaweed green
just-shipped-out green khaki
camouflage green eyes seeing
nothing no more green.

Knew mud & rain. A Seattle
girl knows mud & rain.
But not seeping rain raining
in pores swamping your guts rain.
Not mud that sucks   swallows
boots legs to the knee mud
mud birthing leeches malaria mines.

Knew a year seemed to take   forever
from one birthday to the next. Not time
measured in days marked alive.
Each day a birth a death another day. Fear.

Knew fear of walking
past the line of sixth-grade boys
whistles & barks.
My enemies were all noise
bluster, hope & pimples
& the fights bloodied noses broken
fingers wrestling in the playground.
Once a boy threw a can
of gasoline on another & a match.

Growing up in Jet City I knew
Blue Angel Super Sonic scorched

earth screaming jets. But no bombs
planes people fell
out of my chalk-scrawled skies.

I'd lie on the tall snake green
incandescent rice paddy green grass
next to the post office
on the 4th of July & watch
the night explode. Feel rocket
vibrations, hum of our collective *ahhhh*.

TUESDAY

I wore a thumb-bruise necklace
      around my throat   until
            it dulled yellow

disappeared

my brown bell-bottom corduroys and the pink Tuesday undies I'd
bought
at JCPenney with my babysitting money—

after—*every* Tuesday
plain white   cotton

remember *Tuesday*

embroidered
green   on   pink
polyester torn thrown to the car floor

of the white Chevy
hood ripped
off   engine painted
blood red to lure
a girl
scout like me

a girl
scout squeezing
her brakes gliding   her bike to rest
asking,
do you need help?

      I don't remember
his voice
as if he were drowning

blub   blub   blub

      I do remember/the gun/extended/finger   palm/wrist flicking
they tell me it happens/fast

no
      me
           so
                slow

bike rolling into long grass
front wheel ro ta ting
             so   so slow

      I do remember

thwack   thwack   thwack

from the tennis club down the hill
my mother
playing
with her usual
foursome
mom smacking
her serve
racing the net
      as his gun
             steered me   into the car

glub glub glub kill you glub don't cry
out the window
         wooded winding road gives way
bridge   tunnel   traffic
bus *Big Mac & a Coke* for 99¢

45

we drive into the city maybe my father in his car maybe on the way to
lunch maybe listening to the radio maybe he will see me maybe in his car
dad will listen to the news Nixon maybe he is singing off key *walk on by*
maybe taps his fingers on the dash maybe
a police   maybe   an officer   maybe   if I open this window I will
scream   maybe

we've gone beyond
the city somewhere south
ice cream color houses

the road carved through meadow

                    Chevy heaving up and down the ruts

under
 a maple tree he slows   to a   stop   stop   stop

white broken-down-house-paint-peeling-beyond

now I see

nothing

he says blub blub blub blub
I whisper just a girl just a girl just a girl just a girl only a girl a girl just a girl a girl

brown corduroys slip narrow hips
blue/white striped T-shirt pulled up over

leaving

white cotton undershirt with a little bow at the v

leaving

long legs skinny all bones
                    joints

                sinew that

held me   together

held me   that day

as the man held   a gun

to my head

                held
my body
                    hard under his

held

my thin   throat in his

hand

in time in time   I muscled away
from his hand

away
        from my own sweet scent

girl

AFTERWARD

On Wednesday my mother took me shopping

    after the doctor.
    Just us, honey.
    Anything you want.
      In the changing room,
    Mom blocked
    the mirror with her body
    as I dressed, undressed, dressed,
    undressed, dressed—becoming
    ritual, becoming routine, becoming.

    She smelled of sun lotion,
    peanut butter. I wanted
    her skin, her freckles. I wanted
    her eyes. I wanted
    to smile her smile, eager, wanting
    to fix it.
        I wanted that.

On Thursday, I looked at my body

Sisters gone early to summer camp
I had the bathroom to myself
morning light
washed my body
pink cotton nightgown
puddled by my feet

I leaned into the mirror
saw my neck
red as a plum   swollen

large thumb marks crawled
like beetles up the side

small bruises stained my clavicle
purple   with green edges
paint seeping into paper

stepping back my eyes
looked away from
what they'd seen
looked again

saw my chest   saw skin   white
from my swimsuit top
saw pink nipples
saw   ribs   stomach   summer   brown

until
tan line   white
until
pink   puffy   a torn peony

the doctor said it would   hurt   to   pee
                                hurt   it   hurt

  this girl
in the mirror
this stranger.

On Saturday, I packed my body into a satchel and carried it along with my diary, pjs and toothbrush to my friend Jill's for a sleepover. Late afternoon, we walked down the road, stopped to pick blackberries until our palms, fingers, lips bled red. Wiped juice on our cutoffs before entering Mr. Minota's Corner Store. Screen door slammed behind us, bell jingling. From behind the counter, Mr. Minota nodded our way. Jill steered me to the back, behind the shelves of booze, the magazine stand. An older boy was looking at a *Playboy* inside a *Car & Driver*. He turned away. Jill opened the tobacco case, pulled out a pack of White Owl tipped cigarillos. At the counter, Mr. Minota looked at us, the White Owls. Jill coolly asked for a pack of matches. Maybe he thought they were for her dad. Maybe he didn't care. We walked down to the lake, slipped into the rush along its shore. Sat, feet in the water's wash. Jill knocked a couple of the White Owls from the pack. We bent our heads to the match's spark. Inhaled the White Owl's sad foul smoke, coughed. Coughed what little girl remained.

On Sunday, I came home to the herb
garden, my sisters
who slept like moths in my bed.
The chill
shadow at my elbow—
yellow breath, fresh-scented grass.
The horizon's curve.

FAMILY SECRETS

1

The trees had stopped fruiting years ago,
the orchard reduced, home by home.

My tree was the third one in back, husked
to this patch of land that shouldered

the island's reach into the lake below.
I'd found it at age seven. A running start

to grab the lowest branch with both hands,
swing, then hoist myself up. An easy scramble
to the highest niche. I'd unwrap a sandwich,
pull out my notebook. From there, I could watch

the sailboats kite across the lake, spy
on the neighbors as they barbecued, disappear

into the leaves. Leave my sisters to wonder
if I'd run away with the ice-cream man.

2

I can't tell you
how the lies have piled up
like driftwood after a winter storm,

how I clamber over each log, steady
myself with an outstretched arm
before slipping onto the beach,

how the clear water magnifies
bleached clamshells splayed and split,

how they look like half-moons, reflected over
and over until the seabed's a horizon on Jupiter,

how I long to fill my pockets with shells,
as when we were children, to sell on
our drive's end for pennies,

how our pockets emptied sand, spilled
across the bathroom floor, wet with toe prints.

3
I buried it deep this time. Deeper
than the babysitter's bra, our brother's
Matchbox cars, the ugly photo of me
in glasses and flood pants taken at Long Beach.

I boxed it up last night, the whole
messy story written in disappearing ink
on papyrus, folded into quarters, shoved
into an envelope, stamped with red sealing wax.

I dug all the way to China, with my bare hands.
Dirt under my nails, the telltale.

TEALEAVES

The boy chooses loose tealeaves kept in a square yellow tin handed
down from an aunt who felt a boy with a tea tin would impress a girl.
He scoops leaves into a round sieve on a chain, dangles, then lowers it
into the kettle boiling on the hot plate. Its whistle startles the silence.
He pours tea gently into a porcelain cup, settles it on the saucer with a
grace of lemon. Serves it to the girl who seems unimpressed with the

>tea tin, porcelain cup
>violets dancing on its rim
>moon sliver of lemon,

who no longer desires a cup of tea. But it is teatime he thinks, she came
to his dorm room for this. He palms the crown of her head, lifts the cup
to her closed mouth

>presses lips open
>teacup's hot edge, steam curls
>moistens her nostrils.

Tipping the cup, the tea spills into her mouth. Her eyes tear from the
heat perhaps. Later he will not recall their hue, or the tealeaf clinging to
her lower lip, or the paleness of her face against the rose flush around
her neck as she swallows hard against the burn.

FRESHMAN YEAR

In a few days, I'll be
        myself
               again
        plucking

out poetry on my orange Brother typewriter at my dorm room desk. Out my window, California jaybirds perch in the black oak tree like sapphires in Grammie's brooch. My roommate plays David Bowie's *Golden Years* over and over, beat blending with the hammering of construction across campus.

In a few days, I'll be
        myself,

the doctor says.

Only scars
like traffic arrows
across my thin wrists.

HYPOTHERMIA SURVIVAL GUIDE

The ice underfoot stretches, keens, cracks,
with a thunderclap, breaks open swallowing you.

As you surface, your breath rises to chase.
You have one minute to pace it.

> *I've done this drill. I crawled from a snow shelter*
> *barefoot. My brain a subzero snarl.*

Ten minutes to move before muscle and nerve fibers freeze.
Flutter kick to float. Howl like a dying wolf ensnared.

> *Dead of night. Dead of winter. Dead cold.*
> *Snow shifted into a river around, through my thighs.*

In one hour, you'll lose consciousness.
Before that, you'll have forgotten your name.

> *A girl I barely knew raised to my cry, spooned me*
> *as a lover until my naked body hummed thermal,*
>
> *my eyes blinked open, lips pinked. Nerves lit.*
> *She checked my vitals, my seared skin.*

As your crazy sets in, groan for some body.
Yowl for the sweat, stink of human flesh

to haul you from the suck of dreams pooling,
stripped to a husk, cradled as you burn back alive.

A GIRL'S GUIDE TO THE GALAXY

I hadn't seen stars in ages   sky   tarred with winter's brush
   tonight they turn on   one by one   as if stirred to life by motion
lighting a path home   I could follow it
            build a house in the galaxy
                its milky wonder my milky tea

would I stand on my porch at night   look for Earth—
                for the girl discovering   sea stars in tidal pools
     the woman lying in a field in Bourgogne   inhaling stars
before hitchhiking on to Florence   love waiting   counting on stars
          to guide her up   into a Himalayan night   as the moon
summits Everest   slips into China.
                        time backbends   stretches
     a yogi   centering to nothingness

before exploding—
      a burning starry universe

       from my celestial perch
   I see   myself   raise   my son's finger
               to trace the big dipper   little dipper
         drizzling
           honey   onto this
           and every night.

BEARING FRUIT

At first I wanted to keep you

              like a sweet yellow plum

I picked on a New Hampshire back road
at the slick start of day

blackberries slipping brambles, tar sticky

 as you were at birth

baby boy
        tucking your little wings
                 against the sweat
                     and seep of my milky body

I held you till morning
        to see you in the light that bled
                 through the window

when it came time to name you
cotton-swaddled boy

I scrawled your name
        hesitated
             gave you a father

gave myself away
like the bride I wasn't/was
             mother so happy
             mother to a boy
plucked from the ashes of a fire
forgotten
        with the thought of you angel

wind-spirited
　　lifting
　　　　you ribbon-tailed kite

flight flight flight
　　　　over fruited lands.

THE SQUARE HOUSE
—94 SHAKER ROAD, HARVARD, MASSACHUSETTS

*~Built by Ireland Shadrach in 1769, the Square House
became the center for the Shaker community.*

A square house rooted in a clearing of massive
broadleaf maples that burst into flames each fall.
A house built by a man who skipped the Revolution,
paid the King's taxes, worshipped God.

Neighbors said it was his ghost that lived with us,
the squirrel family in the attic,
hornets nesting in the nursery,
carpenter ants shedding wings, dying,
brittle carcasses scattered like a game of pick-up sticks
and the mosquitos I'd kill at night, creating a monotype
of smashed remains on the bedroom ceiling.

A house with a front door to nowhere,
a swing hung from a lilac bush, the color of cough syrup,
and a cattail-rimmed pond buttered with lily pads,
where I'd take my son to cup tadpoles and skitter bugs.

A house that held strong, my daughter born
during the wail of a late May storm,
rocked her heavy, sleek body mid-night
to the click and whistle of crickets.

GIRL

~For my daughter

Look in the mirror—
do you see what I see?

Girl grown rangy as my plum tree,
its branches escaping over the fence.

Synchronized hearts,
a single bloodstream, singular intent.

I knew nothing then. Not the head-
to-toe sever, rib-to-heart slice

of leavings. Not innuendo's bee sting.
You, girl with dimples pressed

by a god's finger, the corners of a smile gifted
so sparingly.

O to see what I see—a girl
holding steady the breeze between us.

DRESS UP

~A ghazal bouquet

O blooming rose plucked now from my womb, for you I gather
bouquets of pink-lavender-gingham-polka-dotted dresses.

Layered in tissue, awaiting your fat fists to slide through tulip sleeves,
your furry little head to pop peek-a-boo through scallop-collared dresses.

Light snow, New York City children's shop—in the window,
a silk-taffeta-big-back-bow-poinsettia-swirl of a dress.

Boxed and flown home. You wore shiny Mary Janes, delicate snowbell
socks with your kindergarten-Christmas-pageant-dancing dress.

The flower girl flowing down the aisle, a crown of rosebuds,
ribbons kissing the back of your sea-green-tulle dress.

Sixteen, wearing a midnight-silk-organza-prom dress nestled under
peach blossom shoulders. At the gate, you turned, addressed

this moment of wearing a dress, wearing a boy's gardenia, wearing
this skin to play the part I'd given you for our game of dress up.

Crumpled, stashed out of sight, in the back of the closet, my gift to you—
slinky-silk-tie-dyed-fuchsia-teal-yellow-down-to-your-ankles dress.

I saw you in it—all hippy chicky—then saw your face close,
morning glory at night, as you slipped on that dress,

saw how it wore on you, like the lush rose tattoos
that would one day cover you—art undressed.

Secrets wound around us like wisteria—until the petals fell.
I see you now as born, beautiful daughter *sans* dress.

MY CRAFT

—awful scream
                        & I was done

& it was human

it was another boy so like his father &

not *Old soul,* the nurse said the doctor missed

the birth

missed boy & me

my breath willing him
                                his breath catching mine

holding it   tight

eyes open
                flash of fish under water

so strong he lifts his head,
                        looks at me
Mother
                turns
            looks at
                Father

heavy & human

nudges up against my ribs

SMALL DEATHS

The littlest creatures died quickly.
Goldfish lasted days, their glowing orange cadavers
bobbing on the fishbowl's murky surface.

The gecko survived a week. Its carcass
discovered one afternoon
dried up like a bug specimen.

The hamster stayed on earth long enough
to master the spinning wheel to nowhere,
to survive show-and-tell and the squeeze of chubby fists,
before strangulating on the cage bars in a botched escape.

The bunny arrived one Easter then died
days before the next, causing a resurrection watch.
When Hoppy failed to rise from the dead,
his corpse landed in the yard waste.

We never found the cat's body. Banished
to a life outdoors after bloodying the baby's face.
Perhaps it disappeared into the jaw of a ranging coyote.

We were not a family to bury our dead pets
with great ceremony in the back garden
under a handmade cross, whispering prayers

to serve warning to God's small creatures:
Beware. Enter at your own risk.

HOUSEWORK

~ "What pains, what sorrow must I be mothering?"
—Sylvia Plath's "Three Women"

I can't always separate the darks from the lights,
pull the delicate wools out to hang dry.

Sweaters shrink. Blue washes white sheets
to a mid-day summer sky hue.

Sorrow's a word that moans in my mouth
but burrows deep in my chest, a lost sock.

Middle of the night, I hug sadness too close
like children before they leave for college.

And regret—so easily kicked out the throat. Yet
there he is chugging his wood train

across the kitchen floor as I dance
through dinner prep until I learn each step

by heart, the boiling pot raised high.
I scrub worry's fingerprints off walls.

Press out pain, leave the iron hot.
Anger augurs in the oven, a blackberry pie.

Juices seep, then burn and I've forgotten
the delight in their picking. The joy

of finding each plump berry,
thorn pinpricks reminding me I'm alive.

L/ANGUISH

1
Languish.
A Victorian woman languishes on her settee. Plants languish without
water, prisoners in cells, refugees in camps.

An eleven-year-old boy
bolts, bursts, bikes, bothers siblings, swings, swarms & swims.

2
My boy
languishes.
Sleeps in
school
eats less
pizza
pasta
burgers
tacos
hot dogs
chocolate
cake &
ice cream
less & less
until he's
less—a thin
line under
bed covers.
His scalp
scales
nails
arc
gums
bleed
blue

70

eyes
pool.
I dive
in deep.

3

The doctor orders blood tests. A specialist. Hospital.
My boy's immune system has turned
on him. And it fights like a motherfucker.
Shooting wildly, civilian casualties everywhere.

4

My boy's body flares,
flames lick from throat to anus,
he's a house on fire.
We race to the hospital,
a surgeon puts it out.

5

Every day my boy
lays out his arsenal: twenty-four pills.
Swallowed one by one.
Every six weeks
the slow drip into his vein.

6

My boy learns to burn
an angry immune
system to ash.
Embers smolder softly
in his gut.

WAITING IN ARRIVALS

*~Basque Separatists ETA planted a bomb at the Madrid airport
on December 30, 2006*

I pluck glass stars
from my daughter's curls,

sponge the spray of nicks above her brow,
hold her
longer than she desires,
kiss her singing ears.

A bomb
at Barajas airport, buckled
the car park,
killed two men,

rained shards
on my daughter, only waiting

for her friend to arrive,

only   waiting

only

waiting.

ODE TO THE ATHLETE

~With a generous nod to Pindar

Blessed is the boy. Grown tall long
before he'd grown up. Gifted boy,
an unexpected gift. The surprise
of an old soul born easily,
early to parents snared in life's
tragedy. He held fast at first.

Fingers tightly gripped my skirt.
His stories whispered in my ear
alone. Soon, the boy's dreams took flight.
His walk, a run. His jump, a leap.
Phrikias of the preschool set.
Winged feet like Mercury,

he dashed to victory. To best
the boys race after race. His pace quick.
Each year, his share of prizes.
Then felled by injury one day,
wings singed, spirit smoldering,
the boy's mind collected his power.

He took gods' design, made it sweet,
a new beginning for a boy
now becoming a man. His hands
guide his imagination's strength,
reasoning. This race runs faster
at thought's speed. His competition

labors in the city's towers—
lit up at night like captive stars.
He knows the race of men, of gods,
that both breathe life from one mother.

WHAT WE HOLD ON TO

~Dungeness Spit, Washington

The road gathers the fields, harvesting them with each turn.
A barn with silver silos crests the green horizon.
The houses, whose gardens snap sunflowers, rhubarb,
lettuce and stunted corn, are the dream
we each harbor in the folded wing of our palm.

We stem from forest trail to the beach,
skid the sand between our toes,
feel the smooth circles of stone beneath our feet.
This spit is the crooked finger calling the ocean home,
the arm holding our family together.

We sleep on the driftwood,
eat cheese and sausage on Russian rye,
search for agates like four-leaf clovers.
The wind is not enough to unbalance the cranes from their post,
not enough to push us further down the spit to the lighthouse.

HOW COULD WE FORGET?

~For my father

I return every day by kayak, stirring the sun
off the water,
your name lost
among the kelp, your ashes.

Summer evenings—
sun still high
in a periwinkle sky,
you rowed out.
I hauled the crab pot
hand over hand,
seaweed circling my wrists.
You reached into the skittering evergreen mass,
knowing their weight, sex by touch.

We walk the pebbled shore,
crackle clamshells.
Fog hovers—
obscuring the islands,
Olympic Mountains beyond.

WHEN WE WRITE ABOUT THE WEATHER

We write about the weather and yes
                it's about the weather—
                        spring storms lashing

the last life from our winter bones.
                    We are done with it. Yet

relentless rain soaks your poems.
Hurricanes hurl beyond your tight lines.
Form, borders wash into the sea.

If you could reach into the rush of water,
swirl and bounty of it and pull out a heart,
                         would it be yours?

Mine is the yellow tugboat
            dragging a massive barge into the wind.

Surprising physics of grief.

        How ashes float—a sea foam
                of cherry blossom confetti,
                        dusting each wave—
                              disappear with the current.

But I lie.

My heart's adrift on that current
or maybe it's the rock crab scuttling
        sideways along the sea floor searching.

        To lose a father is to lose home.

Sometimes, the buoyant mind becomes a river
claims the land impeding its course to the sea.

Follow it to that scrim of land you claim home.
                    Home, the sea claimed as its birthright.
                        When all is washed away,
                    what remains?

This morning our rain ebbed,
                        weather turned.

AN OYSTER BED

1

When you shuck an oyster, wear a glove
on your left hand. Use a shucker knife

or a strong blade like a Leatherman.
Cradle it with the oyster's hinge

toward your wrist. With your right,
insert the knife tip, press gently till it pops

open. Slip the blade in, creep it along
the right seam to cut the muscle.

2

To eat an oyster, spritz
with lemon, then gently nudge

the meat, awash in brine, with your fork.
Loosened, tip the shell up on your fingers,

tilt to your lips, taste sea,
slip open your mouth and swallow.

3

I learned this trick as a girl.
"You eat oysters with your throat," my father instructed.

We'd hauled a two-gallon steel bucket full of oysters
from beach to dingy to sail boat and now

he steadied it between his knees in our back yard.
I must have been six, maybe seven.

He picked up an oyster with a gloved hand,
shucked it with a knife, lifted it to his mouth.

I watched his Adam's apple, imagined
the oyster slipping down his throat.

My turn. Startle of sea. Brine on my chin.

4
Tonight, I dab each oyster with snail butter teeming
with lemon, Dijon and garlic, parsley, mint from our garden.

Ease them one by one onto the hot grill.
Soon they hiss, spit, the edges slightly browned.

We eat them with charred bread, arugula salad, cold rosé,
gaze toward their birth waters as the sun spills its last light.

SINGLE - HANDED

Hold steady.
Ease into the wind.
I remember my father's
directive—hold a firm tiller
into the wind, sails luffing.

Sail in, come up, catch the wind's
edge. I know to ride its strong thrust,
anger seething along a straining seam
blowing apart, when to fall
off, let the wind
rage on past. To need
no one, to sail solo.

A DRIFT OF FISHERMEN

It was always this way. Sea
edged with ice, lace doilies
crocheted to hold the stones.

Morning black and blue,
the lanterns' light blurs
with the fog lifting ahead of dawn.
A shrug of men, breath casting
ahead as their boats slip shore.

By the time I wake, the boats drift
gray flecks against the horizon.
The men will have emptied
their dreams as they bait, haul and gut.

THE FERRY LINE

That was the moment
he knew he loved her.

Swerving past minivans,
cars, pickup trucks

in the ferry line,
double-fisting triple-scoop

blackberry ice cream cones.
Purple trickles ran

between her bare fingers, flicked
by the summer heat,

dotting windshields, side mirrors
as she ran toward him.

He'd taught her how to ride a bike.
Really ride, clipped in

pedaling light, fast
up the island's hills,

flat out down.
Now he watched her

finish off her cone,
bike balanced on hip,

lick her sticky fingers,
rub them clean down her bike shorts,

lean against her pink handle bars,
look at him with that smile.

CLEAVE

1
It's in the eye,
guiding blade to slice gristle, bone, salvage muscle, meat.
Blood sweats from the cut.

Practiced, I knew how to leave.

2
Root vegetable yanked, grit sustenance.
I ate you, famished.

Now, I cleave—
a curled blossom
in the palm of your body.

WHEN WE FIGHT

I see the sinewy, sienna shoots emerge
from the flesh of his heels, sprout
out of his toes, worm their way through the carpet,
ferret weakness in the floorboards,
crawl under the door to join the insidious
morning glory spreading its violent tentacles
over our lush tended garden.

Meanwhile, I spit out words that flutter
furiously like gypsy moths,
clutter the air around my face.
Their dusty wings powder my hair
before drawing to the light.
Burning bright, singeing wings.

Eventually, I gather up the broken moths,
scatter them like ashes out the window
onto the garden below. He dims the light,
pulls me under the bedding. Limbs
entwined like wisteria vines, our dreams
their fragrant bruised flower.

NOVEMBER 2016

Thanksgiving, and the nasturtiums
are still in bloom. Persimmon

and pomegranate-hued flowers nestle
amongst leaves as large as my hand.

Seeded in the spring in a neat border
edging the grass, along the picket fence—

white, a little worn. My husband
slowly mends the fence, weather

permitting, post by post, slat by slat.
Now, the fence has all but disappeared

in the nasturtiums' tangled brush,
as vines winnowed months ago

under the fence and onto the sidewalk.
Passersby dodge our nasturtiums creep.

Some reach to pluck a bitter flower, take
a bite as they walk on down the road,

their talk of walls and borders, perhaps
just a fence or a bed of nasturtiums.

A CLEAN KITCHEN

Sometimes I worry that the world's got a cold heart. Will it ice over like food left too long in my freezer, little crusts of frost growing fungus under the Tupperware lids? My freezer needs to be cleaned & by that I mean the refrigerator must be cleaned, everything pulled out, shelves wiped & by that I mean the kitchen too, oven, range, cabinets & by that I mean the whole fucking house & the raised beds in the garden need to be planted & the house & the garden where I write at my desk with the dog's dirt & fur curled around my bare toes & the hum of the refrigerator reminding me it wants to be cleaned. I just read a poem from a poet that wants a clean heart, but I want a clean kitchen & a clean poem & I just want our hearts frost free.

WHAT IT'S LIKE TO FALL IN LOVE

I fall in love today
with the man fixing my water faucets,
how he crouches in his boots, feels
his way deftly to salve the leak.
I'm in love with dandelions & ugly bobs
& even morning glory as I yank
their roots free from this dark & luscious soil.
O I love, love the rhododendron
blushing newborn pink, love
the neighbor's rosy plum vine maple
& love the neighbor too,
how she's a dead ringer for Bette Midler
& who doesn't love Bette!
I even love her little dogs—yip & yap.
O today I fall more deeply in love
with my sweet dog, how he rouses
finch & robin from the hydrangea,
barks a greeting at passersby
& they bark back, their people
slowing to lean over our picket fence.
I am in love with strangers today.
Sun brushes foreheads & cheeks.
Shirts & baseball caps rainbow the sidewalk
& smiles curve like tulip petals splayed open.
When bicyclists ribbon yellow, fuchsia, lime
as they flash by, I call out, *I love you!*
O I even love the houseflies flicking
the kitchen window, wanting nothing
more than to escape.

THIS DAY

Live this day as if it's your last is painted on a wall as I run down Broome Street toward the Williamsburg Bridge at 7:30 this morning. The way it was painted black on a sky blue background with flowers & was it Martin Luther King's face? If this is going to be my last day, I am happy I am running & not sleeping in. The day crisp fall, what trees live here aflame. I smile at everyone I pass. I wait patiently for lights to turn, for the policeman to direct the blocked truck along. I am happy because I will soon see my youngest son & be able to hug one of my children on my LAST day on earth & tell him I LOVE him. Then I think about my other children, how I won't be able to hug them. I must call or text ILOVEYOU. Just in case. As I make the turn at the East River & head back to my hotel, I think how my LAST day ever is a day spent in meetings & traveling. Later, I get lost with the Uber driver in an office park & think that those fifteen minutes (almost one percent of this day) were lost too. At least the sun is out & flaming trees line the streets. I am so happy to see my clients & colleagues & hug everyone. I don't tell them I love them (that would be weird) though in that moment & the three and a half hours that follow I feel LOVE. When I arrive at the Newark airport, I am NOT smiling as the TSA Precheck line wraps out past the shops & nearly to the next terminal. This is not good for someone who may not have long to live. To get my head in a LAST-day-on-earth happy space, I talk to the woman in line behind me. I learn about her trip to Tanzania with her daughter. I share my LOVE of traveling with my mother, my daughter. I want to hug her once we reassemble ourselves after TSA (but that would be weird). The ladies' room line is long too. In front of me, a little girl is hopping from foot to foot. I help her mother jump the queue. I want to hug the little girl & her brother. They remind me of my oldest kids when they were little & I want to hug my kids who are now all big & grown up. I have a middle seat & a very large man sitting next to me on the plane. This is not good. I give him my pretzels but no hug. The flight attendant somehow senses that it might be my LAST day & gives me wine, dinner & a movie player for free. I LOVE her, but don't say that, just, thank you thank you thank you. When the plane lands in Seattle, I don't walk, I *run* outside where my husband waits with our dog in the car. I kiss my husband & hold his hand while we drive home. Even though I am on EST & tired, I stay up curled on the couch with him, happy to be home, to be loved, to LOVE, to be alive for this day & all the days that follow.

HOW IT ENDS

1

I think of you. I see our road,
pavement worn, an elephant hide

smudged, yellow line dividing
our coming and going; you,

like the furred grass, shoulders edging
down the sloping hill

to the stone beach. Now I hear the gulls
swooping into the sea.

I've walked beneath the moon's slice
until the jagged glass under

my skin polished sea smooth. You are
my blue washed days.

We untangle our garden
exhale persimmon sun;

the orcas breach.

2

In the woods behind our home
an emptied hornet's nest.

A gossamer paper lantern, we
light a candle, send it burning

into the night. Ah, the hopes of hornets,
you and me. The road ends here.

NOTES

"Âme en Peine à Paris" or "Lost Soul in Paris": *Paris sustained a series of terrorist attacks in 2015, and again in 2016 and 2017.*

"After the Battles" *includes lines from Federico García Lorca's poems "Ghazal for the Dead Child," "Thamar and Amnon," "Landscape with Two Graves and an Assyrian Dog," and "Song of a Little Death" (Farrar, Strauss, and Giroux 2002).*

"Bearing Fruit" *was written for Jack Sinclair.*

"Before and After": *The Gorkha Earthquake, with a magnitude of 7.8Mw, killed nearly 9,000 people and injured nearly 22,000 in Nepal. It leveled large sections of Kathmandu and the villages in the Everest Khumba region, burying climbers at Everest Base Camp.*

"Behind the Wall": *The Berlin Wall separating East and West Berlin was erected in 1961. At midnight on November 9th, 1989, the border was opened, and German unification followed.*

"Beyond": *On December 26, 2004, a tsunami devastated Thailand's Andaman Sea coastline, killing thousands of people and destroying villages.*

"Crash" *came out of a shared family memory.*

"Crossing the Dead Sea": *Israel and Jordan signed a peace treaty on October 26, 1994, opening up their shared border along the Dead Sea.*

"Dissident": *The USSR crushed the Hungarian Revolution of 1956. Hungary continued to live under Soviet rule until the Soviet Union collapsed in December 1991. The book was the forbidden Gulag Archipelago written by Soviet dissident Aleksandr Solzhenitsyn and published in 1974.*

"Earthquake": *The Montenegro earthquake occurred on April 25, 1979 with a 6.9 magnitude. It created over $50 billion in damage, particularly to cultural and* *historical sites. These sites would be damaged again during the war that followed the breakup of Yugoslavia in 1991.*

"Egyptian Erasure": *Taken from Ahmed Abul Ella Ali's blog post written during the Egyptian Revolution, which began on January 25, 2011 and led to the end of Gamal Mubuarak's brutal regime.*

"Get Out": *The fall of 2017 experienced massive natural disasters from earthquakes to hurricanes to forest fires, displacing people and wildlife. Birds sensing impending danger often flee in advance.*

"Girl" and "Dress Up" *were written for Hallie Sinclair. "sans" in Dress Up is French for without.*

"How Could We Forget" *is dedicated to Stephen K. Henkel.*

"How it Ends" *is dedicated to Scott Seaborn.*

"Immolation": *The Arab Spring Revolution started in Tunisia with the self-immolation of Mohamed Bouaziz on December 10, 2010, and spread broadly throughout the Middle East, leading to democratic elections.*

"In Memoriam": *Firefighters died at a forest fire in the Chewuch River Valley, Okanogan County, WA in 2001. There have been numerous fires in this region, which have claimed additional lives of the "smoke jumper" firefighters.*

"L/anguish" *was written for Jack Sinclair, who was diagnosed at eleven years of age with Crohn's Disease.*

"My Craft": *The first three lines came from the last three lines of Ocean Vuong's poem "Essay." It was written for Nicky Sinclair.*

"Ode to the Athlete": *This piece threads lines throughout from Pindar's "Ode to the Athlete," as translated by W.H. Auden (Viking 1955). It was written for Nicky Sinclair.*

"Single-Handed" *is an acrostic of the poet's first and last name.*

"Stop Motion": *Climate change is considered to blame for snow in Michoacán, Mexico, killing migrating monarch butterflies. Photo by Jamie Rojo published in National Geographic in September 2017.*

"Travel Advisory for Turkey": *A series of suicide bombs in 2016 hit tourist areas in Turkey. This was followed by a failed military coup and the resurgence of a strong-arm government state.*

"Waiting in Arrivals": *ETA, the Basque-separatist organization in Spain, planted a bomb in the car park attached to Barajas Airport in Madrid, Spain on December 30, 2006. It blew up, killing two men and injuring hundreds. "Waiting in Arrivals" is about my daughter Hallie Sinclair, who was there.*

"Wandering Seeds": *In the 1600s, the Japanese Edo Empire chose isolationism, while the Ottoman Empire was expanding north, and Europe was setting out to discover new lands.*

"When We Write About the Weather": *was written for poet Matty Layne Glasgow in response to his poems about Hurricane Harvey and Houston.*

"With the Maasai": *East Africa suffered a severe drought in 1984 and has a history of catastrophic droughts that result in livestock displacement and death, and eventually in severe malnutrition and death of people, particularly in Maasai children.*

ACKNOWLEDGEMENTS

My gratitude to the editors of the following magazines and anthologies where these poems appeared, often in earlier versions:

3Elements Review: "Stung"
The American Journal of Poetry: "Crash" and "L/anguish"
Angry Old Man Magazine: "Egyptian Erasure"
Bracken: "Get Out"
Caesura: "The Square House"
Claudius Speaks: "How to Run Away"
Construction: "Beyond" and "Crossing the Dead Sea"
Flexible Persona: "Dissident"
Flypaper: "At the End of Our Marriage, You Contract Congestive Heart Failure"
Freshwater Literary Journal: "Ode to the Athlete"
Fredericksburg Literary and Art Review: "How to Hold a Heart" and "In Memoriam"
Gone Lawn: "When We Write About the Weather"
The Heartland Review: "What I Knew" 2018 Joy Bale Boone Poetry Prize winner
Into the Void: "Small Deaths"
Ithaca Lit: "After the Battles", finalist for the 2017 Lauren K. Alleyne Difficult Fruit Poetry Prize
The Matador Review: "Afterward"
Mississippi Review: "Tuesday" finalist for Mississippi Review Poetry Prize
MORIA: "tealeaves" nominated for Best New Poets, Best of Net, 2018; "Before and After," "Freshman Year," "How it Ends," "I Knew I Had Travelled Far Enough," "Immolation," "Waiting in Arrivals," 2019
The New Guard: "Weather" semi-finalist for Knightville Poetry Prize
Nimrod International Journal of Poetry and Prose: "Family Secrets" semi-finalist for Pablo Neruda Poetry Prize
Penn Review: "Cleave"
Pontoon Poetry: "Stop Motion," 2019
Raven Chronicles: "Single Handed"
Seattle Poetry on Buses: "Off Alki", excerpt from "But How Could We Forget?"

Songs of Eretz Poetry Review: "Âme en Peine à Paris" and "With the Maasai"
Tar River: "Housework"
Timberline Review: "A Drift of Fishermen"
Twisted Vine Literary Arts Journal: "Wandering Seeds" 2018
Vine Leaves Literary Journal: "When We Fight"
West Trade Review: "Finding My Way Home" and "Hypothermia Survival Guide"
Windfall, A Journal of Poetry and Place: "But How Could We Forget?"

"Earthquake" and "How to Run Away" are included in the *Absoloose Vol. 2 Anthology* (Loose Moose 2018).
"November 2016" is included in *Who Want the World Like It Is* (Birds Piled Loosely Press 2017).
"The Ferry Line" is included in the *Ice Cream Poems* (edited by Patricia Fargnoli, World Enough Writers, 2017).
"What We Hold on To" is included in the *Washington 129 Anthology* (edited by Washington Poet Laureate Tod Marshall, Sage Hill, 2017).
"Travel Advisory for Turkey" is included in the *Flying South Anthology* (edited by Steve Lindahl, Winston-Salem Writers, 2016).

"Tuesday" was also a finalist for the International Literary Awards' Rita Dove Award in Poetry 2018.
"Dress Up" was a finalist for the New Millennium Award for Poetry 2018.
"Hypothermia Survival Guide" was also a finalist in the 2016 Cultural Center of Cape Cod National Poetry Competition.
"tealeaves" was also a *Best New Poets* nominee, a *Best of Net* nominee and a Tucson Festival of Books Literary Award for Poetry semi-finalist, 2017.

Some of these poems also appear in the chapbook *Finding My Way Home* (Finishing Line, 2018) and in the political pamphlet *Body Politic* (Mount Analogue Press, 2017).
~
I'm extraordinarily grateful to John Gosslee, Andrew Sullivan, and the entire crew at Mastodon Publishing for creating a publishing home for this book and me.

Immense thanks to the poetic guides that have influenced my work: Kelli Russell Agodon, Lauren Camp, Claudia Castro Luna, Victoria Chang, Kristina Marie Darling, Ishion Hutchinson, Deborah Landau, Robin Coste Lewis, Tod Marshall, Naomi Shahab Nye, Anastasia Renee, Susan Rich, Matthew Rohrer, Maggie Smith, and in particular, David Wagoner, Carolyne Wright and Jane Wong.

I am indebted to Jeffrey Levine, Shanna McNair, Scott Wolven and above all, Veronica Golos for helping shape part or all of this collection with love and a strong eye.

When I started on this journey as a writer in 2016, I found my tribe, and with each year it grows. I am especially grateful to my Hugo House Wagoner workshop, Peter LaBerge and the *The Adroit Journal* staff, Finishing Line Press, my New York University MFA cohort, the Poets on the Coast poets, Tupelo 30/30, Tupelo Truchas and The Writer's Hotel, and above all to my poet sister Lillo Way for companionship in words and heart on this journey.

Thank you to my wonderful global circle of friends and family who have bought books, attended readings, shown up for poetry in ways never imagined, just because.

Finally, it comes to my family: my siblings Page, Muffie and Steve and their families, my children, Jack, Hallie, Nicky and their loves Jenna and Makaela, my mother and (late) father, Denny and Steve, for loving, always, and to Scott where my road ends.

ABOUT THE AUTHOR

Serving as the Chief Communications Officer for the Bill & Melinda Gates Foundation and the European CEO for a major global communications firm, Heidi Seaborn thrived on a degree of chaos—moving 27 times for a career that crisscrossed the globe, with her three children in tow. Along the way, she divorced, remarried, her father died, children grew up and she learned to harness chaos into happiness through love and poetry. Since she started writing in 2016, her poetry has appeared in numerous journals and anthologies including *Nimrod*, *Penn Review*, *American Journal of Poetry* and *The Matador Review*. She's the 2018 Joy Bale Boone Poetry Prize winner and has been shortlisted for over a dozen prizes including the International Literary Awards Rita Dove Award in Poetry, *Mississippi Review* Poetry Prize, New Millennium Prize for Poetry, Wheelbarrow Books Prize for Poetry, Patricia Dobler Poetry Award and Lauren K. Alleyne Difficult Fruit Poetry Prize. She's a New York University MFA candidate, graduate of Stanford University and is Poetry Editor for *The Adroit Journal* staff. She has previously published a chapbook, *Finding My Way Home* (Finishing Line Press, 2018) and a political poetry pamphlet *Body Politic* (Mount Analogue, 2017). Seaborn lives in Seattle on the edge of Puget Sound with her husband and dog. This is her first full-length collection of poetry.

www.heidiseabornpoet.com

MASTODON TITLES

FICTION

A Diet of Worms by Erik Rasmussen
The Pleasures of Queueing by Erik Martiny
Life During Wartime by Katie Rogin

SHORT FICTION

Dead Aquarium by Caleb Michael Sarvis

YOUNG ADULT

Fear to Shred by Joan Gellfend

MEMOIR

Gatsby's Child by Dorin Schumacher

POETRY

Give a Girl Chaos by Heidi Seaborn

SPECIALTY

Manson Family Paper Doll Book by John Reed